What I Know Now

Pamela Hatfield

What I Know Now
Copyright © 2022 by Pamela Hatfield

ISBN: 978-1-949297-59-1
LCCN: 2022905909

All rights reserved. No part of this book may be reproduced, stored in a retrieval system, or transmitted in any form or by any means–electronic, mechanical, digital, photocopy, or any other–without prior permission from the publisher and author, except as provided by the United States of America copyright law.

Unless otherwise noted, all scriptures are from the KING JAMES VERSION, public domain.

Scripture quotations marked (AMPC) are taken from the Amplified® Bible (AMPC), Copyright © 1954, 1958, 1962, 1964, 1965, 1987 by The Lockman Foundation. Used by permission. www.lockman.org

Many of the biblical stories and passages are paraphrased by the author from the King James version.

Address all personal correspondence to:
Pamela Hatfield
PO Box 623
Gilbert, West Virginia 25621

Individuals and church groups may order books from Pamela Hatfield directly, or from the publisher. Retailers and wholesalers should order from our distributors. Refer to the Deeper Revelation Books website for distribution information, as well as an online catalog of all our books.

Published by:
Deeper Revelation Books
Revealing "the deep things of God" (1 Cor. 2:10)
P.O. Box 4260
Cleveland, TN 37320 423-478-2843
Website: www.deeperrevelationbooks.org
Email: info@deeperrevelationbooks.org

Deeper Revelation Books assists Christian authors in publishing and distributing their books. Final responsibility for design, content, permissions, editorial accuracy, and doctrinal views, either expressed or implied, belongs to our authors. It is an honor and a joy for us to help our authors produce works of excellence for the glory of God and the advance of His kingdom.

Table of Contents

CHAPTER 1
Tips for Understanding the Bible 5

CHAPTER 2
God Is LOVE 9

CHAPTER 3
How Powerful Is God? 25

CHAPTER 4
God Wants You to Prosper 31

CHAPTER 5
Why Am I Not Prospering? 41

CHAPTER 6
Jesus Is a Healer 47

CHAPTER 7
What Moves God? 61

CHAPTER 8
Blessings Don't Always Look or
Feel Like Blessings at First 63

CHAPTER 9
Becoming a Christian
Does Not Make You Perfect 73

CHAPTER 10
Persecutions Are Sure to Come 77

CHAPTER 11
You Cannot Believe Everything You Hear 79

CHAPTER 12
Offenses Will Come 81

CHAPTER 13
Parenting Tips 83

CHAPTER 14
Godly Love 87

CHAPTER 15
Jealousy 91

CHAPTER 16
Marital Tips 93

CHAPTER 1

Tips for Understanding the Bible

If you are new to the Bible, let me give you a few helpful suggestions that are quite simple, yet, I believe, will make a tremendous difference in your spiritual growth. I myself wasted many years because I just could not understand a lot of what I was reading, and I didn't want to ask anybody else for help. I didn't have enough sense about me at the time to just ask God to help me understand it. I know there are countless others out there that are just like I was. They have attempted to get to know God, but they have become frustrated and confused and have just given up. I don't want that to be you. There are not words good enough to describe to you what a wonderful difference it will make in your life to really get to know the truth.

First, never doubt and never forget that God is real and that He is the one who is in control of everything. He is the one that will have the final say in everything, no matter what.

Next, before you begin reading the Bible, take the time to say a quick prayer and ask God to keep your mind and heart open and receptive to what He is trying to say to you and to keep you focused on Him and His Word. Ask Him to give you wisdom and understanding as you seek to know Him and don't doubt that He will help you. It is His good pleasure for you to know the truth. Ask Him to heal your mind and spirit of any and all beliefs that you may have that are not true. It's sad to have to say this. But I think we have all been misled or have failed to recognize the truth in some area at some point in our lives.

Next, remember as you read the Old Testament books that we are no longer required to live by the law. We, as Christians today, get the privilege of living by grace through faith in the supreme sacrifice of Jesus Christ. What that means is, if you have placed your faith and trust in Jesus and you are striving to live a holy life, when you make a mistake, and you will make mistakes, it will be atoned for by the blood of Jesus. The law was given to show us that we need a Savior.

Next, never let the devil convince you that you have made too many mistakes or a mistake too horrible for God to forgive you and accept you. He is the master of forgiveness. He knows the more you have to be forgiven for, the more you will love Him when you truly accept that forgiveness. And our love is exactly what He is longing for. Just please be sure you don't take His love and forgiveness for granted. Please show Him the sincere appreciation He deserves.

Next, never forget that Jesus did not come into this world to condemn it (John 3:17). He loves us. He came to save us. He came to help us have the best lives possible. He doesn't want us to go around feeling badly about ourselves or beating ourselves up over our past mistakes. He simply wants us to accept and appreciate His forgiveness and turn from the things that He knows will not bring us peace and joy and happiness. He wants us to leave the past behind. He is not trying to keep us from enjoying our lives. He is doing just the opposite. He is trying to help us enjoy them to the max.

Next, pay attention to whom it is that the writer or Jesus is talking to. If you don't know that, it may seem at times that the Bible contradicts itself. But it never will. If you run into something you don't understand, pause and ask God to help you, and then be still and listen for His answer.

Remember, too, that the different books of the

Bible were written by different men. Sometimes it seems that something is just being repeated. But it is actually different men giving their testimonies about what they witnessed or experienced.

Next, don't rush. Take your time and really think about what God is saying to you. You won't get nearly as much out of it if you just hurry through it. And believe me, you don't want to miss out on anything God has to offer.

Lastly, whatever you do, NEVER STOP SEEKING GOD. Never think you have reached the place where you don't need to spend time in His Word.

CHAPTER 2

God Is LOVE

I believe there are far too many people out there today who are misrepresenting God. They have portrayed Him as this hard, harsh, impossible-to-please Creator. I would like to share with you what I have found to be true.

1 John 4:16 says:

"And we have known and believed the love that God hath to us. God is love; and he that dwelleth in love dwelleth in God, and God in him."

I, personally, spent the largest part of my life believing that God was sitting on His throne in heaven keeping track of each and every mistake we made, and He was going to make sure and certain we got our punishment for every one of them. I always had this notion in the back of my head if you made too many mistakes (and the allowable number was very small), or if you made a really bad mistake, you were going to hell. There would certainly not be any forgiveness for a really bad mistake.

Thankfully, I have discovered that is just not true. Don't misunderstand me. If you refuse to believe the truth that Jesus is the Son of God and that He was crucified on the cross to make atonement for all of our sins and that God raised Him from the dead—if you refuse to accept Him as Lord and Savior of your life, you will be punished for each and every one of your sins. You will go to hell and be in torment for all eternity. But if you will believe the truth and not be ashamed to admit it and strive to live a holy life, it doesn't matter how many mistakes you have made. They will all be covered by the blood of Jesus. You will be forgiven, and God will no longer remember any of your mistakes.

Each of us knows, whether or not we want to admit it, that God is real. The Bible says this in James 2:19:

"Thou believest that there is one God; thou doest well: the devils also believe, and tremble."

If even the devils believe, I know you do, too. The sad thing is, far too many people don't know how good God really is.

I believe there are millions of people out there that still don't quite understand that they don't have to work to earn God's forgiveness. In other words, they don't have to always keep the Ten Commandments (the law) completely and exactly without fail in order to be accepted and loved by God. If that's you, you really need to get this into your heart. The only way you can be right with God is by believing in and relying on the shed blood and resurrection of Jesus Christ. Righteousness is not based on our right actions or behavior. It is based entirely on grace through faith. We cannot earn God's acceptance. We cannot behave well enough to deserve it on our own. We can only accept it as a free gift.

But don't think that gives you a free pass to do just anything you want with no consequences. Hebrews 12:6-9 says this:

"For whom the Lord loveth He chasteneth, and scourgeth every son whom He receiveth. If ye endure chastening, God dealeth with you as with sons; for what son is he whom the father chasteneth not? But if ye be without chastisement, whereof all are partakers, then are ye bastards, and not sons. Furthermore, we have had fathers of our flesh which corrected us, and we gave them reverence: shall we not much more rather be in subjection unto the Father of spirits, and live?"

What that means is, if you are a child of God, when you make mistakes, God will forgive you. But there will still be consequences for your actions. Depending on the circumstances and how hardheaded you want to be, those consequences could be severe, even fatal. He would prefer not to have to chastise us. But He will do whatever is necessary to help us. So, the smart thing to do is to live as holy as you possibly can so you can avoid any undesirable consequences. To be honest with you, you will live a much happier, much more fulfilled life if you do things God's way anyway.

Enough about that; let's get back to the good stuff. Matthew 11:28-30 says:

"Come unto Me, all ye that labour and are heavy laden, and I will give you rest. Take My yoke upon you, and learn of Me; for I am meek and lowly in heart: and ye shall find rest unto your souls. For My yoke is easy, and My burden is light."

I can tell you from my own personal experience that these scriptures are absolutely true. What you will find when you learn of God is that He truly is a God that is full of compassion for you. His heart is full of love for you, no matter how many mistakes you have made. He is gracious, slow to anger, and plenteous in mercy and truth. He will heal everything that needs healing in your life if you will just believe and trust Him and give Him a chance. He actually delights in blessing you.

Isaiah 30:18 (AMPC) says:

"And therefore, the Lord [earnestly] waits [expecting, looking, and longing] to be gracious to you; and therefore, He lifts Himself up, that He may have mercy on you and show loving-kindness to you. For the Lord is a God of justice. Blessed (happy, fortunate, to be envied) are all those who [earnestly] wait for Him, who expect and look and long for Him [for His victory, His favor, His love, His peace, His joy, and His matchless, unbroken companionship]!"

I am still in awe when I think about how good God has been to me after all the things that I have done that displeased and hurt Him. When I finally came to my senses and realized how foolish I had been and how many people I had hurt, I was expecting Him to be really upset with me. But He couldn't have been more loving, compassionate, and understanding. He didn't beat me down and tell me I was no good or just throw me away or anything like that. He didn't even get harsh with me. What He did was tell me to hold my head up and go on.

He wants you to do the same thing. He does not want to hurt you in any way. He simply wants you to turn from the things that He knows will hurt you. When God does chastise you, it's not because He's a control freak or because He is trying to keep you from enjoying anything. It's because He loves you and He doesn't want you to do things that He knows will end up hurting you in the long run. He is on your side. It's like you telling your children not to put their hands in the fire. You try to keep them out of the fire because you don't want them to get burned. You know it will hurt, and you do not want that for them. God is the most loving, kind, compassionate parent there is or ever will be.

Just take a look at what happened to some of the people who chose to make the one true God their God and chose to be obedient to Him. In the book of Ruth, there was a couple that lived in Bethlehem-Judah. The man's name was Elimelech, and his wife's name was Naomi. Due to a famine in the land, the couple and their two sons, whose names were Mahlon and Chilion, left their home and went to the country of Moab to live. While they were there, Elimelech died, and

Mahlon and Chilion married women who were from Moab. One was named Orpah; the other was named Ruth.

Naomi, Mahlon, Ruth, Chilion, and Orpah lived in Moab about ten years. Then Mahlon and Chilion died. At that point, Naomi decided it was time to return home since she had heard that the Lord had blessed her people.

So, Naomi, Ruth, and Orpah started out toward the land of Judah. Along the way, Naomi told both of her daughters-in-law to return to their mothers' houses and blessed them. But they loved Naomi so much, they wanted to stay with her. After a little more persuading from Naomi, Orpah finally returned to her mother's house. But Ruth refused. She stayed with Naomi and decided to make Naomi's God her God.

Naomi and Ruth made it back in the beginning of barley harvest. There was a mighty and wealthy man there who was related to Naomi. His name was Boaz.

One day Ruth went out to glean some ears of corn for her and Naomi to eat. While she was there, the Lord caused Boaz to notice her. He took very good care of Ruth because he had heard that she was very good to Naomi.

Ruth trusted Naomi and followed her advice. Because she did, she became Boaz's wife and bore him a son. All went well for her.

In the book of Esther, you will find that when King Ahasuerus reigned, he made a feast for all his princes and servants. During the feast he sent for Queen Vashti to come before him so he could show off her beauty. But Queen Vashti refused to come, which made the king furious. Because of this, he stripped her of her royal estate and began a search for a new queen.

There was a man named Mordecai, who was a Benjamite, who had raised his uncle's daughter, whose name was Esther, because her mother and father had both died. She was very beautiful and was one of the virgins brought before the king for him to choose from.

Hegai, the keeper of the women, was pleased with Esther so he was very good to her.

At this time Esther had not told anyone who her relatives were because Mordecai had instructed her not to, and she trusted him completely.

When Esther's time came to go before the king, she could have taken anything she wanted to. But she took only what Hegai told her to, and she obtained favor from everybody that looked upon her.

The king loved Esther above all the other women. He sat a royal crown upon her head and made her queen instead of Vashti.

One day Mordecai overheard two of the king's chamberlains plotting to kill the king. He told Esther about it, and she told the king in Mordecai's name. When the king checked the matter out and found out it was true, he hanged both of them and wrote about it in the book of chronicles of the king.

After this, the king promoted Haman above all the princes that were with him. The king commanded all his servants to bow to Haman. But Mordecai would not bow to him because he was a Jew. This made Haman furious, and he started plotting to kill Mordecai. The king did not know that Esther was a Jew, and he made a decree at Haman's suggestion to have all Jews killed.

Esther was grieved terribly when she heard about the decree and looked to Mordecai to help her. He instructed her to go before the king and plead for her people. She knew that whoever went into the inner court without being called risked being put to death. She had not been called for thirty days. Mordecai let her know that being queen would not keep her from being killed if she held her peace and didn't try to help her people. So, Esther and all the Jews in Shushan fasted for three days. They did not eat or drink anything for three days and nights. On the third day, she went to the inner court and found favor with the king.

Once the king found out Esther was a Jew, the Jews were saved, and Haman was hanged where he had planned to have Mordecai hanged. Mordecai was honored for serving the king.

Now let's look at Joseph's story. Joseph was the firstborn son of Jacob (later named Israel) and Rachel. Jacob loved Rachel very much, and he loved Joseph more than all his other children because he was born in his old age. The other children were aware that he loved Joseph more than them, so they were jealous of him and hated him. Jacob made Joseph a coat of many colors and didn't make one for the rest of his children, which made them hate Joseph even more.

One day Joseph's brothers went to feed their father's flock, and Jacob sent Joseph to check on them. When they saw him coming, they conspired to kill him. But his brother Reuben stopped them. Instead, they agreed to put him in a pit in the wilderness. So, when Joseph got to where they were, they stripped him of the coat that his father had made for him and put him in a pit. When they sat down to eat, a bunch of Ishmaelites came by on their way to Egypt. So, they sold Joseph to them for twenty pieces of silver.

To cover up what they had done, they killed a goat and dipped Joseph's coat in its blood and gave it to Jacob. He instantly came to the conclusion that a wild beast had killed Joseph. He grieved and grieved for him.

When Joseph arrived in Egypt, he was sold to Potipher, who was one of King Pharaoh's officers. However, the Lord was with Joseph, and he prospered. He made everything Joseph did to prosper, which caused him to find grace in his master's eyes. Potipher made him overseer of everything he had, and the Lord blessed everything he had for Joseph's sake.

Unfortunately, that caused Joseph problems too. Pharaoh's wife set her eyes on Joseph and tried to seduce him. Because he refused to do such a thing with her, she lied on him and accused him of trying to rape her. This got him put in prison. But the Lord was still with him. He caused the keeper of the prison to favor Joseph and put him in charge of the other prisoners. The keeper didn't even check on what Joseph did because he saw that the Lord made everything he did to prosper.

While there, God gave Joseph the interpretation to two other prisoners' dreams, which eventually caused him to be brought before Pharaoh. Pharaoh saw that the Spirit of God was upon Joseph. So, he put him over all that he had. He gave Joseph a wife, too, who bore him two sons.

Because of a great famine, Joseph's family was forced to rely on Joseph to provide for them. He was eventually reunited with his father and his family, and he provided abundantly for all of them.

Now let's look at Job. He lived in the land of Uz and was an upright man that feared God and shunned evil. He had seven sons and three daughters. He also had several thousand sheep, 3,000 camels, 500 yoke of oxen, 500 female donkeys, and a very big household. He was the greatest of all the men of the East.

One day when his sons and daughters were eating and drinking wine in their oldest brother's house, Job received news that the Sabeans had attacked his servants and taken away all of his oxen and donkeys. Only one servant escaped. While he was still talking, another came and told him the fire of God had fallen from heaven and burned up his sheep and servants there. He was the only one to escape. While he was still talking, another servant came and said the Chaldeans had taken away his camels and slain his servants there. He was the only one to escape to tell Job there. While he was still talking, another came and told him that his sons and daughters were eating and drinking in their oldest brother's house, and a great wind came from the wilderness and destroyed the house and killed his children. He was the only one to survive.

But all of this didn't keep Job from worshipping God. He said he came from his mother's womb naked, and he would return to God the same way. He blessed the name of the Lord anyway.

Then, Satan caused sore boils to come on Job from the crown of his head to the soles of his feet. But he still refused to curse God.

However, Job was still convinced that he was innocent and that he was being treated unfairly until God pointed out to him what he had done. God made it clear to Job that He is a just God and a righteous God and more powerful than anything and everything that ever was or ever will be. But true to His nature, when Job repented, God forgave him and blessed him with over and above what he had to begin with. He now had 14,000 sheep, 6,000 camels, 1,000 yoke of oxen, and 1,000 female donkeys. Plus, he had seven sons and three more daughters. His daughters were prettier than all of the other women in all the land. After that, God blessed him to live 140 more years. Then he died.

Did you notice that in each one of these stories, the people who honored and loved and trusted God and were obedient to Him ended up very successful, very blessed? What that means for you and me is, if you want to be truly successful in life, if you want true happiness and joy and peace to fill your life, the first and most important thing you need to do is to really get to know God. You need to develop a personal, intimate relationship with Him.

You absolutely have to understand that true Christianity is not a set of rules and regulations that you have to keep exactly without error or God's going to get you. It's a loving, compassionate relationship between God and man. God is looking for people who want to spend time with Him because they believe He is good and loving and kind and forgiving. He wants people who know beyond a shadow of a doubt that He is good all the time and that He loves them passionately and is carefully looking out for them. It doesn't matter if you have not reached perfection in your behavior yet; you just have to have a heart that wants to please Him.

With all of that said, here is something that you really need to be aware of and understand. Life is not always going to be a bed of roses and sunshine no matter how hard you try to do good or how well you think you have behaved. You will still be faced with trials and temptations. You will still have to endure difficult circumstances from time to time. Look again at the three examples I just gave you. Each one of them had to endure an incredibly challenging situation. Each one of them experienced sorrow. Ruth lost her first husband. Esther lost both of her parents. And Joseph's own family hated him and sold him into slavery. But the good news is, because they just absolutely refused to doubt that God loved them and that He would work something good out of the situation for them, they all ended up very prosperous, very blessed. That's the way God will be with us, too, if we will trust Him the way they did and keep a good attitude.

When we are faced with difficult or seemingly unfair or painful situations, what we need to do is remember, first and foremost, that God is love, and He is good all the time. If there wasn't something good that we needed in whatever our situation may be, He would not have allowed it to happen. Don't automatically jump to the conclusion that God is mad at you and punishing you for something. He takes no pleasure in having to punish you.

Look at David's life for example. David had to battle a lion and a bear. If you don't know the rest of David's story, you may be asking, how could having to battle a lion and a bear possibly be beneficial to anybody? Turns out it was very beneficial for David. Those two encounters strengthened his faith that the Lord would protect him. They prepared him for his battle against Goliath. He knew as long as he did what God was asking of him, God would back him up and give him the victory. He knew that nobody or nothing could defeat Almighty God.

The lesson we all need to learn from all of this is this: if you will continue to trust God no matter what, there will be a great reward at the end of the journey. Whatever you have had to go through will certainly be worth it in the end if you keep believing right.

CHAPTER 3

How Powerful Is God?

God is so powerful that He just spoke, and heaven and earth came into existence. He is so powerful that He not only created light (the sun and moon and stars), but He also divided the light from the darkness, too. He created every creature on the earth. He formed man out of the dust of the ground and breathed into his nostrils, and he became a living soul. He appeared to Moses in a flame of fire out of the midst of a bush and kept the bush from being consumed. He turned Moses' rod into a serpent and then back into a rod again. He turned his hand leprous and then back to normal. He turned the water into blood. He made frogs cover the land of Egypt. He turned dust into lice. He made swarms of flies to cover the land of Egypt and kept them from the land of Goshen where His people were. He killed all the cattle of the Egyptians and kept alive all that belonged to the Israelites. He made boils to come upon all the Egyptians. He caused very grievous hail to fall on the Egyptians and kept it off of His people. He made locusts devour the land of Egypt. He made a thick darkness that could be felt to cover Egypt for three days. But all the children of Israel had light. He killed all the Egyptians' firstborns but spared all of the Israelites'.

He led His people by a pillar of a cloud by day and a pillar of fire by night. He made the waters of the Red Sea part and let the Israelites cross the sea on dry ground. Then He drowned all the Egyptians with the same water. He turned the bitter water to sweet for His people to drink. He caused quail to come to the desert to their camp so they would have flesh to eat. He sent them manna to eat for forty years. He made water to come out of a rock. God is so powerful that when He descended upon Mount Sinai, the whole mountain quaked greatly. God is so powerful that the people of Israel were afraid to hear Him speak. They were afraid they would die if they heard His voice.

Exodus 24:17 says:

"And the sight of the glory of the LORD was like devouring fire on the top of the mount in the eyes of the children of Israel."

God is so powerful that when Korah, Dathan, Abiram, On, and 250 princes of the congregation revolted against Moses and Aaron, He caused the earth to open and swallow Korah, Dathan, Abiram, and their wives, sons, little children, all that belonged to them and all their goods and then closed the earth upon them. Then He consumed the 250 princes with fire (Numbers 16).

God is so powerful that He cast down great stones from heaven and killed more of the army of the five kings of the Amorites than the Israelites killed themselves. Then He caused the sun and moon to stand still until Israel had finished destroying them (Joshua 10).

God is so powerful that when He commanded Ezekiel to prophesy to a valley of very dry bones that they would live, He caused the bones to come together, bone to his bone where they belonged. Then He made the sinews and flesh come upon them. Then He covered them with skin. Then He told Ezekiel to prophesy to the wind to come from the four winds and breathe upon the slain so they would live. And they lived and stood upon their feet (Ezekiel 37).

God is so powerful that when they put Daniel in the lions' den, He sent an angel and shut the lions' mouths so they could not harm Daniel. After Daniel was kept unharmed because he believed in his God, King Darius commanded that the men that had accused Daniel and their children and their wives be cast into the den. The lions broke all of their bones in pieces (Daniel 6).

God is so powerful that He kept Shadrach, Meshach, and Abednego from being harmed when they were cast into a burning, fiery furnace. They refused to bow down and worship the image of gold that King Nebuchadnezzar had made. So, the king commanded that the furnace be heated seven times more than usual. The fire was so hot that it killed the men that took Shadrach, Meshach, and Abednego up to it. God protected Shadrach, Meshach, and Abednego. Not one hair of their heads was singed. None of their clothes were changed or burned. They didn't even have the smell of smoke on them (Daniel 3).

God is so powerful that He brought Lazarus, who had been dead and in his grave for four days, back to life (John 11).

God is so powerful that even the beasts, birds, and animals obey His voice. He had the ravens take bread to Elijah to eat (1 Kings 17).

He is so powerful that He had Elijah build an altar in His name. He had him make a trench around it and put wood on it, then a bullock. He then had him fill four barrels of water and pour them on the bullock and wood. He did that three times, equaling twelve barrels of water. He filled the trench with water, too. Then the fire of the Lord fell and consumed the bullock and the wood and the stones and the dust; it even licked up the water that was in the trench (I Kings 18). That's pretty powerful to consume even the stones.

He even caused Abraham, who was 100 years old, and Sarah, who was 90 years old, to conceive and bear a child (Genesis 21).

This is one of my personal favorites. God is so powerful that He caused the enemies of Judah to destroy one another. Not one of them escaped, and the people of Judah didn't have to fight at all (2 Chronicles 20).

As impressive as all of this is, this is just a fraction of the power of God. There is nothing He can't do except lie.

What I Know Now

CHAPTER 4

God Wants You to Prosper

I believe far too many Christians today are living way below what God desires for them. I can't tell you how many times I have heard people quote Matthew 19:23-24:

"Then said Jesus unto His disciples, Verily I say unto you, That a rich man shall hardly enter into the kingdom of heaven. And again I say unto you, It is easier for a camel to go through the eye of a needle, than for a rich man to enter into the kingdom of God."

The problem with this is, they don't seem to remember that the scriptures go on to say this in Matthew 19:26:

"But Jesus beheld them, and said unto them, With men this is impossible; but with God all things are possible."

If you will read Mark's account of this incident, which is found in Mark 10:17-27, I believe you will understand this a little better. There was a man that came running to Jesus, who kneeled to Him and asked Him what he should do that he may have eternal life. Jesus told him that he knew the commandments, such as do not kill, do not steal, do not bear false witness, defraud not, honor thy mother and father. He told Jesus he had observed all these things from his youth. Jesus answered and said he lacked one thing. He told him to go and sell all that he had and give to the poor, and he would have treasure in heaven. And then he should come and take up his cross and follow Him. The man was sad at that saying and went away grieved because he had great possessions.

The real problem wasn't that he had great riches; it was the fact that he loved and trusted in his riches more than he did Jesus. Matthew 6:24 plainly states that you cannot serve God and mammon (money).

I believe what He was trying to get across to them was that if a person becomes rich before they have been born again, they tend to develop a love for material things rather than Jesus and become self-reliant.

They tend to have a hard time letting go of what they think they earned themselves, not realizing that God could have taken everything they have obtained in the twinkling of an eye. They don't seem to realize that it was God's grace all along that enabled them to obtain what they have obtained. Therefore, it is extremely difficult for them to surrender their lives to God. Not only that, but rich people generally also have too many distractions to keep them from really developing a close personal relationship with Jesus.

To be honest with you, I used to fear becoming rich because of that scripture. But the more I have studied and meditated on God's Word, the more my mind has changed about that. As you have already seen in the examples I have given you, God obviously doesn't mind us having nice things at all as long as we love Him and not the material things. He really wants us to be blessed so that we can be a blessing to others.

Just think about this for a little bit. Proverbs 10:22 says:

> *"The blessing of the LORD, it maketh rich, and He addeth no sorrow with it."*

If God didn't want us to be rich, why would His blessing make us that way?

Psalm 35:27 says:

> *"Let them shout for joy, and be glad, that favour My righteous cause: yea, let them*

say continually, let the LORD be magnified, which hath pleasure in the prosperity of His servant."

2 Corinthians 8:9 says:

"For ye know the grace of our Lord Jesus Christ, that, though He was rich, yet for your sakes He became poor, that ye through His poverty might be rich."

3 John 1:2 says:

"Beloved, I wish above all things that thou mayest prosper and be in health, even as thy soul prospereth."

Psalm 1:1-3 says:

"Blessed is the man that walketh not in the counsel of the ungodly, nor standeth in the way of sinners, nor sitteth in the seat of the scornful. But his delight is in the law of the LORD; and in His law doth he meditate day and night. And he shall be like a tree planted by the rivers of water, that bringeth forth his fruit in his season; his leaf also shall not wither; and whatsoever he doeth shall prosper."

Deuteronomy 28:1-14 says:

"And it shall come to pass, if thou shalt hearken diligently unto the voice of the LORD thy God, to observe and to do all His commandments which I command thee this day, that the LORD thy God will set thee on high above all nations of the earth: And all these blessings shall come on thee, and overtake thee, if thou shalt hearken unto the voice of the LORD thy God. Blessed shalt thou be in the city, and blessed shalt thou be in the field. Blessed shall be the fruit of thy body, and the fruit of thy ground, and the fruit of thy cattle, the increase of thy kine, and the flocks of thy sheep. Blessed shall be thy basket and thy store. Blessed shalt thou be when thou comest in, and blessed shalt thou be when thou be when thou goest out. The LORD shall cause thine enemies that rise up against thee to be smitten before thy face; they shall come out against thee one way, and flee before thee seven ways. The LORD shall command the blessing upon thee in thy storehouses, and in all that thou settest thine hand unto; and He shall bless thee in the land which the LORD thy God giveth thee. The LORD shall establish thee an holy people unto Himself, as He hath sworn unto thee, if thou shalt keep *the commandments of the LORD thy God, and walk in His ways. And all people of the earth shall see that thou art called by the name of the LORD; and they shall be afraid of thee. And the LORD shall make thee plenteous in goods, in the fruit of thy body, and in the fruit of thy cattle, and in the fruit of thy ground, in the land which the LORD sware unto thy fathers to give thee. The LORD shall open unto thee His good treasure, the heaven to give the rain unto thy land in His season and to bless all the work of thine hand: and thou shalt lend unto many nations, and thou shalt not borrow. And the LORD shall make thee the head, and not the tail; and thou shalt be above only, and thou shalt not be beneath; if that thou hearken unto the commandments of the LORD thy God, which I command thee this day, to observe and to do them: And thou shalt not go aside from any of the words which I command thee this day, to the right hand, or to the left, to go after other gods to serve them."*

Matthew 7:11 says:

"If ye then, being evil, know how to give good gifts unto your children, how much

more shall your Father which is in heaven give good things to them that ask Him?"

If you read through the entire Bible, you will see time after time that the people who believed in and trusted and were obedient to God ended up prosperous. In the twenty-first chapter of John, you will see that Jesus' disciples had been out fishing all night and had caught nothing. But when morning came, they saw Jesus standing on the shore. He asked if they had any meat. They answered that they hadn't. He told them to cast the net on the right side of the boat, and they would find them. When they did what He told them to do, they were not able to draw the net in for the multitude of fish in it.

God considered David a man after His own heart. Acts 13:22 says:

"And when He had removed him, He raised up unto them David to be their king, to whom also He gave testimony, and said, I have found David the son of Jesse, a man after Mine own heart, which shall fulfill all My will."

Also, look at what Scripture says about him in 1 Chronicles 29:28. It says:

> *"And he died in a good old age, full of days, riches, and honour: and Solomon his son reigned in his stead."*

Solomon honored God, too. Look at what the Bible says about him. 2 Chronicles 9:22 says:

> *"And king Solomon passed all the kings of the earth in riches and wisdom."*

Look at what the Bible says about Abraham. Genesis 24:34-36 says:

> *"And he said, I am Abraham's servant. And the Lord hath blessed my master greatly; and he is become great: and he hath given him flocks, and herds, and silver, and gold, and menservants, and maidservants, and camels, and asses. And Sarah my master's wife bare a son to my master when she was old: and unto him hath he given all that he hath."*

Look at what Job 1:1-3 says:

> *"There was a man in the land of Uz, whose name was Job; and that man was perfect and upright, and one that feared God, and eschewed evil. And there were born unto him seven sons and three daughters. His substance also was seven thousand sheep,*

and three thousand camels, and five hundred yoke of oxen, and five hundred she asses, and a very great household; so that this man was the greatest of all the men of the east."

So, do you see that God really does want you to have good things? You don't have to be crooked, underhanded, or greedy to prosper. What you should be doing is trusting God and being obedient to Him and not loving money.

But please keep this in mind. I don't want you to get discouraged if you don't step into your blessings immediately. You may have to go through some challenging times, just like Joseph did, before you receive your blessings. You may have some character flaws that God needs to help you with before He can give you what He wants to. So, just be grateful for all the blessings that you have already been blessed with. And whatever comes your way, just don't doubt God's goodness, and you will eventually get the rest of them.

What I Know Now

CHAPTER 5

Why Am I Not Prospering?

You may be asking the question, "Why am I not prospering?" The answer may surprise you. It could be that you are just not spiritually mature enough to handle prosperity just yet. Believe it or not, having plenty of money can hurt you more than it helps you at times. God cares way too much about you to give it to you if He knows that is going to be the case.

I assure you. It is not because He does not want you to have good things. It's not because He loves somebody else more than He does you. You are the apple of His eye. He just wants you to love Him instead of material things, and you will never be able to do that unless you really get to know Him.

It could be that you just don't believe that God wants you to prosper, like I used to. I hope the chapter you just read will change your mind about that. I believe you will begin to see wonderful things start to happen if it does.

It could be that you just need to change the

way you think and talk. Do you realize that when you say things like nothing good is ever going to happen to you, what you are doing, in essence, is calling God a liar? Well, it is, and I am pretty sure He doesn't particularly like it when we call Him that.

I know it's extremely easy to get negative when you experience one disappointment after another. Especially when you don't realize that you have done anything wrong to bring about the seemingly bad things that are happening to you. But we really need to be extremely careful not to start talking negatively about our lives and our futures. We need to remember during those seasons that all things work together for good for those who love God and are called according to His purpose (Romans 8:28). Just because something doesn't seem good at the time doesn't mean that it isn't.

We need to be more like Job. He experienced a great deal of disappointment in his life. Yet, he remained unwilling to curse God and came out of his trial with more than he went into it with. We need to remember that God is a just and righteous God and keep our hearts and minds open to Him and repent when He points out a fault to us.

Let me ask you a question. Do you believe that

God is love and that He is good all the time? I used to think I did. I even wanted to. But the sad truth was I really didn't. Like so many others, I encountered some really bad things at a very young age. And, I just couldn't understand at the time why, if God was so good, He would allow those horrible things to happen to me.

Thankfully, He has helped me to understand things a little better now. He helped me to realize that He knows the end from the beginning. He knows everything that is going to happen before it ever does. He knows every thought you think. He knows every dream you dream. He knows how He made us. He knows each and every one of our strengths. He knows each and every one of our weaknesses. And He knows the desires He has put in our hearts.

He also knows that in order for us to be truly compassionate toward others and effective at helping them, we need to know where they are and what they are going through. We need to know what they are thinking and feeling. Unfortunately, sometimes the only way for us to really know that is to experience it ourselves. He also knows what we are going to need in the future. It has been extremely helpful and healing for me to come to that understanding and to know that God was not punishing me for something I didn't deserve to be punished for.

Just like David, God wasn't punishing me by allowing the things He allowed. He was preparing me for the battles, the challenges, and the opportunities that I would be facing in the future. He was equipping me with the knowledge and compassion that I would need in the future. I am sure that's the case for you, too.

Let me ask you another question. Are you seeking the kingdom of God and His righteousness first? Or does something else have first place?

Matthew 6:33 says:

"But seek ye first the kingdom of God, and His righteousness; and all these things shall be added unto you."

God is a good God, and He cannot lie. If you will just seek Him first and foremost and aim to do things His way, He will take care of you. He will bless you.

Remember, God owns it all and controls it all.

I believe there are numerous people who don't believe God will do the things for them that He did for the people in the Bible. Please believe me when I tell you this: that is an outright lie. God does not respect or care for any one person more than He does another. It does not matter to Him whether you are rich or poor, black or white, skinny or fat. Anything He did for one, He will do for you if you will just believe and not doubt it.

Do not let the devil rob you of your blessings any longer. Dare to believe that God loves you just as much as He does any other human. And be expecting to see His goodness and blessings overtake you. I believe you will be amazed at what will happen if you will.

What I Know Now

CHAPTER 6
Jesus Is a Healer

This is just my personal opinion. But I believe Jesus wants to heal each and every one of us of any and all illnesses or diseases that we may have. Just look at all the people He healed in the scriptures.

Matthew 8:1-3 says:

"When He was come down from the mountain, great multitudes followed Him. And behold, there came a leper and worshipped Him, saying, Lord, if Thou wilt, Thou canst make me clean. And Jesus put forth His hand, and touched him, saying, I will; be thou clean. And immediately his leprosy was cleansed."

Mark 1:23-26 reads:

"And there was in their synagogue a man with an unclean spirit; and he cried out, Saying, Let us alone; what have we to do with Thee, Thou Jesus of Nazareth? art Thou come to destroy us? I know Thee who Thou

art, the Holy One of God. And Jesus rebuked him, saying, Hold thy peace, and come out of him. And when the unclean spirit had torn him, and cried with a loud voice, he came out of him."

Matthew 8:14-17 reads:

"And when Jesus was come into Peter's house, He saw his wife's mother laid, and sick of a fever. And He touched her hand, and the fever left her: and she arose, and ministered unto them. When the even was come, they brought unto Him many that were possessed with devils: and He cast out the spirits with His word, and healed all that were sick: That it might be fulfilled which was spoken by Esaias the prophet, saying, Himself took our infirmities, and bare our sicknesses."

Matthew 9:27-30 reads:

"And when Jesus departed thence, two blind men followed Him, crying, and saying, Thou Son of David, have mercy on us. And when He was come into the house, the blind men came to Him: and Jesus saith unto them, Believe ye that I am able to do this? They said unto Him, Yea, Lord. Then touched He their eyes, saying, According to your faith be it unto you. And their eyes were opened; and Jesus straitly charged them, saying, See that no man know it."

Mark 2:3-12 reads:

"And they come unto Him, bringing one sick of the palsy, which was borne of four. And when they could not come nigh unto Him for the press, they uncovered the roof where he was: and when they had broken it up, they let down the bed wherein the sick of the palsy lay. When Jesus saw their faith, He said unto the sick of palsy, Son, thy sins be forgiven thee. But there were certain of the scribes sitting there, and reasoning in their hearts, Why doth this man thus speak blasphemies? Who can forgive sins but God only? And immediately when Jesus perceived in His spirit that they so reasoned within themselves, He said unto them, Why reason ye these things in your hearts? Whether is it easier to say to the sick of the palsy, Thy sins be forgiven thee; or to say, Arise, and take up thy bed, and walk? But that ye may know that the Son of man hath power on earth to forgive sins, (He saith to the sick of the palsy,) I say unto *thee, Arise, and take up thy bed, and go thy way into thine house. And immediately he arose, took up his bed, and went forth before them all; insomuch that they were all amazed, and glorified God, saying, We never saw it on this fashion."*

Matthew 12:10-13 reads:

"And, behold, there was a man which had his hand withered. And they asked Him saying, Is it lawful to heal on the sabbath days? that they might accuse Him. And He said unto them, What man shall there be among you, that shall have one sheep, and if it fall into a pit on the sabbath day, will he not lay hold on it, and lift it out? How much then is a man better than a sheep? Wherefore it is lawful to do well on the sabbath days. Then saith He to the man, Stretch forth thine hand. And he stretched it forth; and it was restored whole, like as the other."

Luke 7:11-16 reads:

"And it came to pass the day after, that He went into a city called Nain; and many of His disciples went with Him, and much people. Now when He came nigh to the gate of the city, behold, there was a dead man carried

out, the only son of his mother, and she was a widow: and much people of the city was with her. And when the Lord saw her, He had compassion on her, and said unto her, Weep not. And He came and touched the bier: and they that bare him stood still. And He said, Young man, I say unto thee, Arise. And he that was dead sat up, and began to speak. And He delivered him to his mother. And there came a fear on all: and they all glorified God, saying, That a great prophet is risen up among us; and, That God hath visited His people."

Matthew 9:18-25 reads:

"While He spake these things unto them, behold, there came a certain ruler, and worshipped Him, saying, My daughter is even now dead: but come and lay Thy hand upon her, and she shall live. And Jesus arose, and followed him, and so did His disciples. And, behold, a woman, which was diseased with an issue of blood twelve years, came behind Him, and touched the hem of His garment: for she said within herself, if I may but touch His garment, I shall be whole. But Jesus turned Him about, and when He saw her, He said, Daughter, be of good comfort; thy faith hath made thee whole. And the woman was made whole from that hour. And when Jesus came into the ruler's house, and saw the minstrels and the people making a noise, He said unto them, Give place: for the maid is not dead, but sleepeth. And they laughed Him to scorn. But when the people were put forth, He went in, and took her by the hand, and the maid arose."

Mark 7:32-35 reads:

"And they bring unto Him one that was deaf, and had an impediment in his speech; and they beseech Him to put His hand upon him. And He took him aside from the multitude, and put His fingers into his ears, and He spit, and touched His tongue; And looking up to heaven, He sighed, and saith unto him, Ephphatha, that is, Be opened. And straightway his ears were opened, and the string of his tongue was loosed, and he spake plain."

Luke 22:50-51 reads:

"And one of them smote the servant of the high priest, and cut off his right ear. And Jesus answered and said, Suffer ye thus far. And He touched his ear, and healed him."

John 5:2-9 reads:

"Now there is a Jerusalem by the sheep market a pool, which is called in the Hebrew tongue Bethesda, having five porches. In these lay a great multitude of impotent folk, of blind, halt, withered, waiting for the moving of the water. For an angel went down at a certain season into the pool and troubled the water: whosoever then first after the troubling of the water stepped in was made whole of whatsoever disease he had. And a certain man was there, which had an infirmity thirty and eight years. When Jesus saw him lie, and knew that he had been now a long time in that case, He saith unto him, Wilt thou be made whole? The impotent man answered Him, Sir, I have no man, when the water is troubled, to put me into the pool: but while I am coming, another steppeth down before me. Jesus saith unto him, Rise, take up thy bed, and walk. And immediately the man was made whole, and took up his bed, and walked: and on the same day was the sabbath."

John 9:1-7 reads:

"And as Jesus passed by, He saw a man

which was blind from his birth. And His disciples asked Him, saying, Master, who did sin, this man, or his parents, that he was born blind? Jesus answered, Neither hath his man sinned, nor his parents: but that the works of God should be made manifest in him. I must work the works of Him that sent Me, while it is day: the night cometh, when no man can work. As long as I am in the world, I am the light of the world. When He had thus spoken, He spat on the ground, and made clay of the spittle, and He anointed the eyes of the blind man with the clay, And said unto him, Go, wash in the pool of Siloam, (which is by interpretation, Sent.) *He went his way therefore, and washed, and came seeing."*

Matthew 4:23-24 reads:

"And Jesus went about all Galilee, teaching in their synagogues, and preaching the gospel of the kingdom, and healing all manner of sickness and all manner of disease among the people. And His fame went throughout all Syria: and they brought unto Him all sick people that were taken with divers diseases and torments, and those which were possessed with devils,

and those which were lunatick, and those that had the palsy; and **He healed them** [emphasis by author]."

Luke 6:17-19 reads:

"And He came down with them, and stood in the plain, and the company of His disciples, and a great multitude of people out of all Judaea and Jerusalem, and from the sea coast of Tyre and Sidon, which came to hear Him, and to be healed of their diseases; And they that were vexed with unclean spirits: and they were healed. And the whole multitude sought to touch Him: **for there went virtue out of Him, and healed them all** [emphasis by author]."

Matthew 12:15 reads:

"But when Jesus knew it, He withdrew Himself from thence: and great multitudes followed Him, and **He healed them all** [emphasis by author]."

Luke 9:11 reads:

"And the people, when they knew it, followed Him: and He received them, and spake unto them of the kingdom of God, and healed them that had need of healing."

Luke 4:40 reads:

"Now when the sun was setting, all they that had any sick with divers diseases brought them unto Him; and **He laid hands on every one of them, and healed them** [emphasis by author]*."*

And the list goes on. It is up to you to believe it and receive it.

If you need healing, the following are some scriptures that you can meditate on that may help bring your healing to pass.

Exodus 23:25 reads:

"And ye shall serve the LORD your God, and He shall bless thy bread, and thy water; and I will take sickness away from the midst of thee."

2 Chronicles 7:14 reads:

"If My people, which are called by My name, shall humble themselves, and pray, and seek My face, and turn from their wicked ways; then will I hear from heaven, and will forgive their sin, and will heal their land."

Psalm 34:17 reads:

"The righteous cry, and the LORD heareth,

and delivereth them out of all their troubles."

Psalm 103:1-5 reads:

"Bless the LORD, O my soul: and all that is within me, bless His holy name. Bless the LORD, O my soul, and forget not all His benefits: Who forgiveth all thine iniquities; who healeth all thy diseases; Who redeemeth thy life from destruction; who crowneth thee with lovingkindness and tender mercies; Who satisfieth thy mouth with good things; so that thy youth is renewed like the eagle's."

Psalm 147:3 reads:

"He healeth the broken in heart, and bindeth up their wounds."

Proverbs 4:20-22 reads:

"My son, attend to my words; incline thine ear unto my sayings. Let them not depart from thine eyes; keep them in the midst of thine heart. For they are life unto those that find them, and health to all their flesh."

Isaiah 53:5 reads:

"But He was wounded for our transgressions, He was bruised for our iniquities: the

chastisement of our peace was upon Him; and with His stripes we are healed."

Jeremiah 30:17 reads:

"For I will restore health unto thee, and I will heal thee of thy wounds, saith the LORD; because they called thee an Outcast, saying, This is Zion, whom no man seeketh after."

Jeremiah 33:6 reads:

"Behold, I will bring it health and cure, and I will cure them, and will reveal unto them the abundance of peace and truth."

Acts 10:38 reads:

"How God anointed Jesus of Nazareth with the Holy Ghost and with power: who went about doing good, and healing all that were oppressed of the devil; for God was with Him."

James 5:14-15 reads:

"Is any sick among you? let him call for the elders of the church; and let them pray over him, anointing him with oil in the name of the Lord: And the prayer of faith shall save the sick, and the Lord shall raise him up;

and if he have committed sins, they shall be forgiven him."

1 Peter 2:24 reads:

"Who His own self bare our sins in His own body on the tree, that we, being dead to sins, should live unto righteousness: by whose stripes ye were healed."

3 John 2 reads:

"Beloved, I wish above all things that thou mayest prosper and be in health, even as thy soul prospereth."

What I Know Now

CHAPTER 7

What Moves God?

The one thing that moves God is faith in His goodness. Any time you need a prayer answered, it is vital that you attach some faith to it when you say it, or you might as well just not say a prayer at all.

Matthew 21:21-22 (AMPC) reads like this:

"And Jesus answered them, Truly I say to you, if you have faith (a firm relying trust) and do not doubt, you will not only do what has been done to the fig tree, but even if you say to this mountain, Be taken up and cast into the sea, it will be done. And whatever you ask for in prayer, having faith and [really] believing, you will receive."

James 1:6-7 (AMPC) reads like this:

"Only it must be in faith that he asks with no wavering (no hesitating, no doubting). For the one who wavers (hesitates, doubts) is like the billowing surge out at sea that is blown hither and thither and tossed by

the wind. For truly, let not such a person imagine that he will receive anything [he asks for] from the Lord."

Another important thing you need to remember is this.

Mark 11:25-26 says:

"And when ye stand praying, forgive, if ye have ought against any: that your Father also which is in heaven may forgive you your trespasses. But if ye do not forgive, neither will your Father which is in heaven forgive your trespasses."

CHAPTER 8:

Blessings Don't Always Look or Feel Like Blessings at First

I cannot tell you how many times in my life that I have thought that either God wasn't real, or if He was, there must be something wrong with Him. But I have to tell you, I have discovered that there never was and never will be anything wrong with God. He knows exactly what He is doing at all times, and everything He does is for our benefit.

The preaching I heard growing up had me too fearful of God. I was so scared that I was going to do or say something wrong, and God was going to be mad at me. I was so afraid that I really couldn't get anything out of the Bible when I did try to read it. And to be honest with you, I really wasn't all that interested in getting to know Him because I never thought I'd be able to please Him.

However, God did prove to me that He knows everything about me and that He knows exactly what He is doing at all times. Although it didn't make sense or seem good at the time, He still did something wonderful in my life.

I generally try to be easygoing and understanding of others. It usually takes a lot to really make me mad. However, God knows that when I do really get mad, I kind of lose it. Fear goes completely out the window. In those moments, I would likely try to fight King Kong. So, this time He made me mad. I remember sitting on my back porch and saying how I didn't know how in the world anything good could come out of this. I have been through this junk so many times. Finally, I looked up into the sky and asked, "God, why do You hate me?"

Much to my surprise, His answer to me was, "Get in the Book and find out." Needless to say, I didn't have to ask what book He meant. I knew instantly that He meant the Bible. That was exactly what I did. As soon as I started reading His Word, my fear was gone, and guess what I found out... God didn't hate me at all. He had every right to, and He should have, but He didn't. Just the opposite was what I found: God loved me!

I am happy to tell you that I am no longer afraid to read the Bible. In fact, God has healed me of all sorts of fears since that time. The peace and hope that He has given me are priceless. That turmoil I used to be in moved me to a place where I began to see God as He really is. I could not be more pleased that He showed me the truth.

So, no matter what you may be going through, or have been through, just know in your heart and absolutely refuse to doubt that God does, in fact, love you, and whatever He does choose to allow to come your way is for your good. Something good will come out of it if you will continue to trust His love for you and His goodness.

I can assure you of one thing. If you will make the choice, and you do have a choice, to believe that God is LOVE and that He loves you individually, personally, and unconditionally (faults and all) no matter what may come to pass in your life, your life will begin to be so much better. You will start to see things happen that you just can't put a price on.

I remember one time just before my husband had to quit work. He worked on a strip mining job, and he took care of all the ditches. He usually got up around 2:30 in the morning to start getting ready for work, and he usually didn't get back home until around 5:30 in the evening. This particular day, he was really tired when he got home. He had just been home long enough to take a shower and sit down to dinner.

While he was eating, the phone rang. It was his boss wanting him to come back out and work all night. They had had a problem with one of the ditches that day, and as luck would have it, the inspector showed up just after he left and threatened to shut the whole job down if it wasn't fixed by the next day. They didn't have anybody else there at the time who could get it fixed. So, it was my husband or no one.

As tired as he was, he couldn't stand the thought of all those other men going without a payday. I tried and tried to get him not to go, but he insisted. He grabbed a thermos of coffee and something to eat and headed back out. If all of that wasn't bad enough, it was rainy and foggy out that night too, which made visibility even worse. It broke my heart to see him leave, but God was right there for me.

Just after he left, the phone rang again. It was my aunt this time. She had tried to call my mom and couldn't get an answer. Before she hung up, I asked her to pray for Billy. When I got off the phone with her, I went to my mom's house to check on her. She was okay. When I told her about Billy, she called her pastor and his wife, and they prayed for him.

When I got back to our house, as I was walking

through the door, I felt the presence of the Lord so strongly in our house. I don't think I have ever felt it that strongly before. When I left the house, I had left my television on. When I walked into the living room, my eyes were drawn to the TV screen. Right there in black and white were the words "Everything's gonna be all right." You can call that a coincidence if you want to, but I know beyond a shadow of a doubt that was the hand of God reaching out to me.

That was God's handwriting on the wall, so to speak. That's just the kind of God He is. He doesn't want us to worry and fuss and fret and be depressed. He wants us to know that with Him, everything is going to be all right. And by the way, everything was all right. The ditch was fixed. Everybody kept working, and Billy made it back home safely.

Looking back at this incident, it didn't seem like a blessing at first. But the way God showed up for me and comforted me and protected Billy increased my faith. I know that, as tired as Billy was before he left the house, even with the coffee, there is no way possible that he could have kept that piece of machinery on the side of that mountain that night and drove for two more hours to get home the next morning without an accident. I know it was God that enabled him to do that.

But even better than that, it proved to me that God really does care about me. He doesn't want me to worry or be sad, and He doesn't want that for you, either.

Look at the story of Joseph. At first glance, you wouldn't think that being put in prison for something you didn't do would be a blessing at all. Most of us, I think, would be sorely displeased and heartbroken, to say the least. But when you get to the end of his story, you realize that that was indeed a blessing. God used that experience to heal him of the character flaw that he had so it wouldn't be a problem for him in the future, and it put him in the position to be promoted. Had Joseph not been there in the prison, Pharaoh would not have known that God would give him the interpretation to his dream, and Joseph would not have been promoted to second in command and control of everything that Pharaoh had.

Look at the story of King David. Once again, you wouldn't think, at first glance, that being attacked by a lion and a bear would be a blessing at all. But it actually was just that. Those two incidences gave him the courage to fight the giant Goliath and win, which in turn, put him in the king's seat.

Another incident that happened to me that

didn't seem good at first was the time I was walking along the riverbank, and the ground gave way beneath me. My leg went down into a hole that the water had evidently washed out beneath the surface. I remember thinking immediately when I saw the hole that it looked like a snake's den so I got my leg out of it as quickly as I could. I remember it felt like I scratched my leg on something when I pulled it out of the hole.

It didn't really bother me until the next morning when I was getting ready for work. I noticed there was a dark, round spot about the size of a fifty-cent piece just above my knee, and when I ran a razor across my leg, it hurt like heck. The whole top portion of that leg was that way. I was so upset I didn't know what to do. So, I prayed and asked God what I was supposed to do. I needed to be at work in about 30 minutes. The answer I heard was, "Put something over it so nothing can scratch it, and it will be okay." So, that's what I did.

While we were having lunch, I told three of my coworkers about it. My supervisor looked at me and said, "I would be going to the emergency room." I just laughed. I knew if God said it would be okay, it would be okay. I was right. It was okay.

I think God allowed that to show them that His power is real and to increase my faith at the same time. It also let me know that He is carefully watching after me and nothing that may come my way is beyond His control.

Then I had some sort of growth come up on the upper part of my stomach. I'm still not sure exactly what it was. I just know that it wasn't normal. I hadn't paid much attention to it because it hadn't really caused me any problems. Not long after I noticed it, the church we were attending had communion, and I participated.

The following Friday, I was walking through my living room, and that growth started stinging a little. So, I started looking at it every couple of hours or so. Each time I looked at it, it looked a little darker. By bedtime, it looked black. So, I decided to put a bandage over it to make sure I didn't scratch it or anything in my sleep. When I took the bandage off the next day, that growth fell right off with it. There was nothing left but pink, healthy skin.

Once again, that just let me know that God does care. It had to be the communion that caused that to fall off because I hadn't done anything out of the ordinary besides that.

So, I just want to encourage you a little bit here. If you find yourself in a position that you are not particularly happy with at first, just remember how God operates. Remember, if you will keep the faith and a good attitude toward God, He will bring something really good to pass for you.

What I Know Now

CHAPTER 9

Becoming a Christian Does Not Make You Perfect

I believe there are a lot of people out there that think if you profess Christianity, you should never make a mistake. They automatically judge someone they do see make a mistake as a hypocrite. It is true that you should strive to be as holy in your actions as you can. But let me take the pressure off of you a little bit. The best of us on our best day are not going to be perfect and completely sinless until this life is over. I know there are some out there who like to think they are and like to act like they are. But don't let them fool you. I assure you; they are not. They still have flaws and weak areas just like the rest of us do.

I used to think that people that had the baptism in the Holy Spirit and spoke in tongues were holier than I was in their behavior. But that has not always been the case at all. God took me on a journey to several different places and had me observe several different people. What I discovered was that each one of those people still had flaws too, even the preachers. I discovered it was more a matter of what they believed than it was their actions.

The point I am trying to get across is this: you should never attempt to judge whether or not someone is a true Christian. Only God and the individual know that for certain. You should keep in mind that people are human and sometimes their minds get confused. Sometimes when they get really tired or stressed out, their minds just don't seem to function properly. Sometimes they just mindlessly get caught up in something. Sometimes they develop chemical imbalances in their bodies that cause their minds to malfunction. Sometimes, they have just not come to the realization that something they are doing is not right is God's eyes. Christianity is not an instant cure for everything that is wrong with you. It is a growing process.

With all of that said, let me point out one more thing. If you do happen to see someone who professes Christianity do something that you don't think is right in God's eyes, remember that God in Philippians 2:3 encourages us to esteem or regard others as better than and superior to ourselves. That means we should correct the behavior with gentleness and love and compassion and encouragement. It is not your duty or God's will for you to condemn them or put them down.

Let me repeat that just to make sure you get it. It is not your duty or God's will for you to condemn them or put them down. If you want to do what is right and help them, pray for God to enlighten them to the truth and help them to repent and encourage them not to give up or quit. Show them that God loves and will forgive them if they will just repent. Do what you can to help them succeed instead of trying to trample them down. Treat them like they truly are better than and superior to you.

Can you just imagine how much better our world would be if we would all start doing that?

What I Know Now

CHAPTER 10

Persecutions Are Sure to Come

Do not make the mistake of thinking that your character will not be attacked when you start living the way God wants you to live and treating others the way He wants you to treat them. Satan will do whatever he can to keep you and everybody else from growing spiritually and from walking in all the blessings that God wants to bless you with. He is not your friend. He is a liar and the father of all lies, and he certainly doesn't want you to persuade anybody else to become a Christian.

If you discover that people have started vicious rumors and lies about you when you are doing the best you can to live a holy life and being good to others, you should take it as a compliment instead of an insult. Don't let them upset you. God has your back. He is a God of justice. Hold your head up and be proud. You must be doing something really good for God, or Satan wouldn't be against you. Remember, he only attacks those who are doing him harm. So, keep up the good work and don't get discouraged. You are on the verge of something great. If you will keep pressing forward, there will be a great reward for you.

What I Know Now

CHAPTER 11

You Cannot Believe Everything You Hear

Proverbs 14:15 reads like this:

"The simple believeth every word: but the prudent man looketh well to his going."

We really need to be careful what we choose to listen to, especially where God is concerned. Like I said before, what I listened to growing up had me believing some things that were not true at all, and it really did a lot of damage. I believe the people I listened to really had good intentions at heart, and they really thought they were speaking the truth. But now I realize that they were just as mistaken as I was. So, I strongly encourage you to take a little time to seek God's face for yourself and ask Him to reveal anything in your beliefs that is not true. It will make a tremendous difference in your life to find these things out. It sure has in mine.

From what I have experienced, you really can't believe a lot of what you hear about other people either. For one thing, when a person gets jealous of somebody else, their eyesight seems to malfunction. They start to see things in a completely distorted way. Sometimes people will even build somebody up just to get them out of their hair and into somebody else's. Then you have people who think they have something to gain by distorting the truth about somebody else, so they do. Sometimes people are afraid to tell the truth because they have been threatened or they fear they will be left alone. And there are some people out there who think it's funny to tell tales and stir up trouble between people. So, always be cautious and use your own judgment.

You really need to be careful not to believe negative things that are said to you. Try to keep in mind that people are human, and they are flawed. They make mistakes. Even if it's somebody you respect, if it's negative, don't listen to it. A lot of times, people will get upset and say things that they really don't mean at all. If you are not careful, those things will sink down into your belief system and cause you all sorts of problems. Try to always remember that you are valuable to God, and He loves you. So, there must be some good inside there.

CHAPTER 12

Offenses Will Come

Don't make the mistake of thinking that a member of the church will never hurt you. You have to keep in mind that other Christians still have flaws and weaknesses, too. None of us are beyond having a bad day, saying or doing something foolish or being hateful. The devil knows that there is no hurt in the world like being hurt by a brother or sister in the church. So, naturally, he is going to try to cause as many offenses as he can through someone within the church.

Just remember when these situations happen, it is not God trying to run you away. It is the devil at work trying to keep you from growing and maturing and receiving all of the things that God has for you.

Be determined in your heart not to let these offenses upset you. Be determined to stay in there and fight for your blessings. Be quick to forgive whoever offended you and pray for God to bless them and help them. Keep in mind that you still have flaws and weaknesses, too, and you still need others to pray for you and support you, too. In doing so, you help yourself. What you do for others, God will do for you.

If you do not think that's true, pay attention to this. Not too long ago, I was having some very painful problems with my back. So, I asked the church to pray for me. Before the service was over, the preacher asked if anybody had a testimony. The woman sitting in front of me did. She was one of the women that prayed for me. She said she knew I had been healed because she had been having problems with her back, too. As she was praying for me, she felt a cool sensation go down her back, and it was healed, too. Thank God, my back was healed and not hurting any more.

CHAPTER 13

Parenting Tips

From what I have witnessed over the years, there are two main areas that cause the worst problems with children.

First, a lot of parents just seem way too eager to punish their children for every little mistake they make. I believe most of them honestly think they are doing what is right and good because they have heard people say if you spare the rod, then you spoil the child. Don't misunderstand me and think I don't want you to correct wrong behavior in your children, because I absolutely do. But from what I have witnessed, and I have spent a great deal of time around children, is most of the time, the behavior could be corrected without the punishment.

I believe children are born with a natural desire for their parents to love them and be proud of them. I have witnessed children whose parents are never around, and you can see that void in their hearts. But when a child is constantly being put down, quarreled at, and punished, they soon lose that desire, and the trouble really begins. So, I just want to encourage you. When you do need to correct some behavior in your child, for your sake and the child's, please try to be more understanding. They are just children, and they don't understand everything. They can't help the flaws that they came into the world with. So, make sure that you correct them in a way that is uplifting and encouraging and helpful. Make sure that they can see the love in your correction and know that you want good things for them. I promise you; you will be glad you did.

Then, there are those who have children who have experienced some form of tragedy in their lives. It may be that one of their parents has left and is no longer around or a death of someone they were close to. Instead of helping them to deal with it and encouraging them to be positive, they go overboard pampering them and start blaming everything they do wrong on somebody else. Please believe me when I tell you this: if that is you, you are not helping your child. You are hurting them. I have seen this scenario played out too many times. It always ends in disaster.

If you want to be a good parent, and I believe you do, please teach your child how to cope with disappointments in a healthy, positive way. Children are usually a lot tougher than you think they are. Keep reminding them that God will work something very good out for them through the situation if they will keep believing right and keep a good attitude and be patient. Most importantly, pray for them and have other believers you know pray for them. Remember, "The effectual fervent prayer of a righteous man availeth much" (James 5:16).

What I Know Now

CHAPTER 14

Godly Love

1 Corinthians 13:1-8 says:

"Though I speak with the tongues of men and of angels, and have not charity, I am become as sounding brass, or a tinkling cymbal. And though I have the gift of prophecy, and understand all mysteries, and all knowledge; and though I have all faith, so that I could remove mountains, and have not charity, I am nothing. And though I bestow all my goods to feed the poor, and though I give my body to be burned, and have not charity, it profiteth me nothing. Charity suffereth long, and is kind; charity envieth not; charity vaunteth not itself, is not puffed up, Doth not behave itself unseemly, seeketh not her own, is not easily provoked, thinketh no evil; Rejoiceth not in iniquity, but rejoiceth in the truth; Beareth all things, believeth all things, hopeth all things. Charity never faileth: but whether there be prophecies, they shall fail; whether there be tongues, they shall cease; whether

there be knowledge, it shall vanish away."

Charity in this sense is another word for love. We should love others the way God loves us. We should always be eager to think kindly of others and be eager to try to help them.

Let's break this down a little bit and see if there are any areas that we need to do better in. You don't have to advertise your weak areas to everybody. But I do encourage you to be honest with yourself, and if you realize you do have an area that needs improvement, pray and ask God to help you in that area. He is always willing and eager to help us if we will just ask and believe.

Do you remember what the scriptures just said? If you have not charity, you are nothing. I don't know about you. But I don't want to be nothing.

First, Scripture says charity suffereth long and is kind. Now, ask yourself this question. When I see a fault in someone else, am I patient and kind and encouraging and helpful with them? That is how love would be. Or am I quick to get agitated and condescending with them?

Next, charity envieth not. When I see someone who seems to be more successful than I am or seems to have better qualities than I do, am I truly happy to see them succeed and supportive of them? That is how love would be. Or am I resentful or jealous of their success and secretly looking for ways to sabotage it?

Next, charity vaunteth not itself, is not puffed up. Do I have a humble spirit and give God the honor and glory for all the good things in my life? Or do I act proudly, like I am somewhat better than others who don't seem to be quite as successful or talented or pretty as I am?

Next, charity does not behave itself unseemly. Do I treat others the way I would like to be treated? Do I treat them with respect? That is what love would do. Or do I tend to have one set of rules for me and another set for other people?

Next, charity seeketh not her own. Now, ask yourself this question. Do I go about my day looking for ways to help or encourage others? That is what love would do. Or is my primary focus on what I would like myself?

Next, charity is not easily provoked. Does it take a lot to really get me upset? That is how love would be. Or am I quick tempered and easily offended?

Next, charity rejoiceth not in iniquity, but rejoiceth in truth. Now ask yourself this question. Am I happy to tell the truth if it means I will not get what I would like? That is how love would be. Or would I lie if it meant I would get what I wanted?

Next, charity beareth all things. Now ask yourself this question. Do I bear with others through thick and thin? That is what love would do. Or am I only a "good-time" pal?

Next, charity believeth all things. Now ask yourself this question. Do I always try to believe the best of others? That is what love would do. Or am I eager to think the worst?

Next, charity hopeth all things. Now ask yourself this question. Do you hope for the best for others? That is what love would do. Or do you set about to make sure nobody gets a foot above you?

Finally, charity endureth all things. Now ask yourself this question. Do I stay in the fight until it's over? That is what love would do. Or do I turn my cheek and quit after a certain point?

I hope you aced this test. But if not, please don't get discouraged. Just keep trying to do better. I still need a little work myself.

CHAPTER 15

Jealousy

$\mathcal{S}$ong of Solomon 8:6 says:

"Set me as a seal upon thine heart, as a seal upon thine arm: for love is strong as death; jealousy is cruel as the grave: the coals thereof are coals of fire, which hath a most vehement flame."

The way I see it, this scripture could not be truer. Jealousy is one of the most horrendous attributes I believe a person can have. The sad thing is that even the people that you would least expect to be jealous of anybody are consumed by it at times.

People seem to lose all sense of morals and sensible reasoning when jealousy kicks in. Many of them seem to think they are helping themselves by starting vicious rumors and lies about the person they are jealous of or by doing whatever they think they can to keep that person from succeeding. But let me assure you, just the opposite is true. You will never get ahead by trying to tear somebody else down. You may succeed for a while, but it will ultimately do you more harm than good.

The really sad part of all of this is that jealousy is utterly senseless to begin with. God has not done anything for one person that He isn't willing to do for you. It's not His fault that somebody else has more than you do. It's the choices that we have made for ourselves that have put us in the situation that we are in. So, instead of doing what you can to beat somebody else down, why don't you simply start making better choices for yourself? Why don't you do what you can to help as many other people as you can succeed? The good you do for others will always be returned to you, and it is usually multiplied when it returns.

CHAPTER 16

Marital Tips

I don't believe there is a man or woman, either one, that doesn't want to know that he or she is married to a person that they can trust with any and everything. I believe that in order for them to feel that way about you, you have to have your mind made up that you are going to do what honors God in all situations. You need to let them see that. Please trust me when I tell you this. God rewards obedience. He will honor your commitment to Him and cause your spouse to have eyes only for you. I am not saying that you will never experience difficulties or have disagreements. But the bottom line is this: they will love you.

If you are a woman, do not let the devil deceive you into thinking that dressing provocatively will keep your husband's eyes on you. It will only create problems for you in the long run. Honor God at all times and dress modestly. In other words, make sure that all the important parts are covered at all times except for your alone time with your spouse.

Do not try to provoke your spouse to jealousy. It will get old to them, and they will lose interest.

Pray for your spouse on a regular basis and always encourage them to do what is holy and right in God's eyes. Like I said before, God rewards obedience.

Always encourage your spouse to trust God's love for them. I promise you; your life will be so much better and so much happier if you will.